KEYS TO KEEP YOUR MARRIAGE WORKING

THE ULTIMATE GUIDE TO ENJOY A GOOD AND HEALTHY MARRIAGE

Eric Medvedev

Table of content

Chapter 1

What is Love?

Friendship, physical attraction, intellectual compatibility, and, of course, love itself are all essential elements of a successful relationship. Love is the glue that holds a relationship together. How can you know if you're in love, and what exactly is love?

It is difficult to define true love because everyone's interpretation of it might differ drastically. People frequently conflate lust, attraction, and companionship. As a result, there is no one perfect way to define love.

A deep sense of joy and intense enthusiasm for someone or something is a more succinct definition of love. Probably, this definition or meaning of love does not encompass all the emotions that makeup what it feels like to be in love.

Is love an emotion? Yes.

How would you sum up love?

Love is a feeling that is a combination of many different feelings. Love means giving yourself and others a chance, not rushing, being patient, being kind, not being envious, and not having expectations. Although it has historically been employed as a noun, love is a verb.

It is about what we do for others and the various ways we foster a sense of love and concern for those around us. Love has changed over the years and centuries, just like most other things in the world. Love wasn't always as we understand it today.

When it comes to a union between two people back then, love was either secondary or even not a factor. Marriages, which are regarded as the culmination of a romantic relationship in several cultures and regions of the world, were typically transactional. People choose whether or not to get married based on whether or not the union would benefit them financially and politically.

However, if we examine artistic genres like poetry, it appears that people have been experiencing love for a very long period.

A comprehensive sensation, love. Love can be defined by many different things, including words and deeds. One extremely common question we may ask is, "What is love, and what isn't?" What love means in a relationship is likely a common question.

Being in a relationship does not imply being in love. Even if you have a strong sexual attraction to your spouse, it does not necessarily follow that you know what love is. If you haven't built a solid foundation of love with your partner, you'll lose interest after the sexual chemistry fades.

A loving relationship takes time to develop. It takes time for the strands of love to come together and form a solid connection. Love can only grow when you and your spouse talk about your feelings, worries, dreams, and hopes. So be patient with love and trust the process. It needs to be respected and not rushed because it has its schedule.

We talk of finding our soul mates, but people are capable of falling in love repeatedly. Thank goodness, else we wouldn't ever get over having a crush in high school or losing a relationship to divorce or death.

Self-esteem and confidence can be boosted by the sense of unwavering love, acceptance, independence, and security that come with a strong relationship. It also lessens stress, which is a factor in many mental health issues including anxiety or depression.

Qualities of True Love

1. Care
One of the fundamental components of love is care.
If we love someone, we will be concerned about their feelings and general welfare. To ensure their wellbeing, we might go above and beyond, even sacrificing our wants to meet theirs.

2. Compliment
In relationships and love, admiration is essential.

One may admire someone for their physical appearance or even for their intelligence and character. A fundamental component of love is accepting another person's opinions and liking them for who they are on the inside and out.

3. Desire
Desire can be both physical and mental, as well as sexual.

Being around someone, wanting them, and simply wanting to spend more time with them are all components of the desire you experience when you fall in love.

What is love not?

It's crucial to understand what love is not when we talk about the components of love and what love is. We frequently mistake other emotions or feelings for love, but eventually, we realize that the way we feel about a particular individual is not loving.

Lust is not love.
Despite the idiom "it was love at first sight," we don't always feel love.

Do you know that intense need to be drawn to someone you just met, almost like a magnet? That is chemistry and infatuation. Mother Nature provides us a healthy amount of infatuation to initially bring us together. Sexual chemistry is a part of love, but love is different since love is an emotion that takes time to develop. While love develops over time as you get to know the other person on the inside and out, lust can erupt in an instant.

Being in a relationship does not imply being in love. Even if you have a strong sexual attraction to your spouse, it does not necessarily follow that you know what love is. If you haven't built a solid foundation of love with your partner, you'll lose interest after the sexual chemistry fades.

A loving relationship takes time to develop. It takes time for the strands of love to come together and form a solid connection. Love can only grow when you and your spouse talk about your feelings, worries, dreams, and hopes. So be patient with love and trust the process. It needs to be respected and not rushed because it has its schedule.

We talk of finding our soul mates, but people are capable of falling in love repeatedly. Thank goodness, else we wouldn't ever get over having a crush in high school or losing a relationship to divorce or death.

Although it is merely an emotion, people might display indicators of being in love. By what they do for you, what they say to you, and how they act around you, you can tell if someone is in love with you.

1. Love is giving
In a genuinely loving relationship, we give to one another without anticipating anything in return. We don't keep track of who provided what for whom. It makes us happy to make our partner happy.

2. Love entails compassion

The joy we get when we witness our partner's happiness is the ultimate definition of love. We experience their downcast mood when we observe them be gloomy or depressed. Empathy for the emotions of the other person comes with love.

3. Love entails giving in

The true definition of love in a relationship is willingly putting your wants second to those of your spouse.

But we don't give up ourselves in doing this, and neither should the other person demand that we give up ourselves for their benefit. That is abuse and control in a relationship; that is not what love is all about.

4. Courtesy and respect

So, when we are in love, we treat one another with kindness and respect. We never purposefully harm or disparage our partners. The listeners can feel the affection in our words when we speak of them while they are not around. We never disparage our allies behind their backs.

5. We behave morally and ethically
Woman removing I love you sticky note off the mirror

We can behave properly and ethically with them and in our community because we love them. They inspire us to become better individuals so that they will still find us admirable because they are in our lives.

6. We protect one another's privacy.
Even when we are alone, love keeps us from feeling lonely. We experience a constant sense of presence from our

guardian angel just by thinking about the other person.

7. Love means not tolerating jealousy
After a lot of effort, when our partner wins, we beam with pride as if we had also won. There is only genuine joy in witnessing our spouse thrive; there is no sense of competitiveness or jealousy.

8. We never stop thinking about them.
Even when we are apart because of jobs, travel, or other obligations, our minds occasionally wander to them and what they might be up to "right now."

9. Intimacy increases sexually
Love makes sexual activity sacred. Our lovemaking today is deep and holy, a true union of bodies and minds, in contrast to the early days.

10. Feeling secure

Winter romance between a man and a woman.
Love makes it possible for us to feel protected and secure as if the other person is a safe harbor for us to return to. We experience stability and security while we are around them.

11. We feel heard and seen
Even after accepting us for who we are, our partner still loves us. We can display both our good and bad aspects while yet receiving their undying affection.

They are aware of who we truly are. We can reveal our souls to love and get grace in return.

12. Love encourages fearless combat
What is the essence of love? It is a feeling of safety.

We can dispute and know it won't end our relationship if we are confident in our love. We don't keep grudges against our partner for very long since we don't like to harbor ill will toward them, therefore we agree to disagree.

Love is a really strong feeling. As a result, it may affect us in both positive and harmful ways. These repercussions of love might be psychological, emotional, or even physically manifest. True love has the power to transform us.

Your body, mind, and well-being can be adversely affected by unhealthy, unrequited love and terrible relationships.

Love can affect people's mental health in both positive and negative ways, as was described in the section on the effects of love.

Self-esteem and confidence can be boosted by the sense of unwavering love, acceptance, independence, and security that come with a strong relationship. It also lessens stress, which is a factor in many mental health issues including anxiety or depression.

On the other hand, unhealthy relationships that are toxic from the start or become toxic over time can result in insecurities that go beyond the partnership and have an impact on a person's mental health and future romantic relationships.

One may feel less than they are when they believe they are not doing things correctly, are not good enough, or are unable to live up to expectations.

Abandonment difficulties can develop that affect more than simply the relationship if somebody leaves abruptly, cheat, or lie.

Chapter 2

What is Marriage?

Marriage is the union of a mature man and woman who are in a romantic relationship and have decided to become husband and wife. It is a full agreement between the two lovers to live together as one.

However, a marriage's success is influenced by a variety of variables. In a marriage, it's important to accept one another, argue fairly, appreciate one another, communicate, and do other things. By understanding what marriage is and what its most important elements are, you may learn how to take advantage of being married and build a solid marital connection.

The dynamics of a romantic relationship and those of marriage don't change all that much. But with time, there has been a

notable change in what spouses expect from one another, among other things.
Being somewhat aware of what marriage means to you can help you prepare for such changes and maintain a healthy relationship. It will also help you work toward developing solid habits. Equally important to consider before choosing a marriage are a few things:

- wisdom gained from experiences
- make sure that you and your spouse share the essentials and looking for a funny partner
- never accept less than what you can receive

What obligations should one fulfill before getting married?

Marriage is undoubtedly one of life's biggest commitments. Every marriage takes a lot of work from everyone involved for it to prosper.

There are a few things to take care of before getting married, including understanding what marriage implies, setting up a communication system, sharing a list of things you wouldn't like to compromise on, and so forth.

It's imperative to talk about several important matters and pose questions to your partner before you go down the aisle. You can adjust and grow to know one another better as a result.

Chapter 3

What does a good and healthy marriage mean to you?

Even if a marriage unites two spirits, each couple has their idea of what a successful partnership entails. A successful and healthy marriage is hard to define precisely. But here are some conventional definitions of a successful and content marriage.

1. Having a trustworthy wife
Some individuals think that a happy marriage depends on having a good wife. Some people believe that a moral wife who will always defend and support her husband is necessary for a happy marriage.

2. Training moral kids
Some individuals believe that being married brings a couple's family together. They

believe it is their duty as parents and as members of society to nurture morally upright kids. They believe that raising their children well will be a sign of a successful marriage because it will produce better citizens for society.

3. Having strong communication abilities.
Some people believe that companionship and efficient communication are crucial elements of a successful marriage. These people genuinely feel that open communication and full sharing of all personal details are essential for a successful marriage.

4. Sharing a home
This could be the easy trick to a happy marriage if you're looking for one. One of the most frequently used descriptions of a successful marriage is this. Some people believe that maintaining close connections is the key to a successful marriage.

5. Unconditional love and understanding

Other prevalent characteristics of an effective marriage are dedication, responsibility, and sacrifice. Some people believe that unwavering love and respect for one another are the keys to a successful marriage. Accept your spouse as they are and acknowledge that everyone has imperfections.

Chapter 4

However, for you to keep your marriage working, here are some vital keys to achieving that. These keys will help you build a good and healthy marriage.

Keys to enjoying a good and healthy marriage;

1. Interaction

No matter how you feel about it, good communication is essential for a great marriage. Always be sure to communicate your expectations and desires. Keep in mind that effective communication is crucial to a happy marriage.

2. Respect

Respect in a marriage should be shared. Marriage may be nasty and painful if there is no respect. Getting rid of everything that can your spouse treat you disrespectfully, or vice versa would be in your best interest. Recognize your partner's perspective and make an effort to be sympathetic.

It's a great idea to respect your spouse's right to hold contrary opinions while still being able to comprehend them.

3. Establishing Limits

Setting up distinct personal boundaries is a necessary component of a good marriage. Make time for yourself and remain true to who you are. Even if you go on dates five days a week, you should still make time to visit your friends and family frequently.

4. Trust

Both parties must have complete and mutual trust for a marriage to succeed. You must make an effort now, even if it takes time to develop that kind of trust.

5. Encourage
Every good and healthy marriage has a faithful spouse. It is crucial to have a spouse that believes in you wholeheartedly.

6. Work on listening intently.
We must speak. Did you know that the best strategy for a good and healthy marriage is to create a space for open communication? Most couples are reluctant to admit this.
We stress that men should give special attention to this area, even though all women should practice active listening. Men frequently merely need to be a listening ear for their partners. This is

the result of their upbringing and socialization, respectively.

Keep in mind that hearing and listening are two distinct processes. Our hearts are involved in listening. Open yours, pay attention, keep your eyes on her when she speaks, and you might even paraphrase to reassure.

The essential key to having a good and healthy marriage—and, by extension, to every relationship—is listening.

7. Accept disagreement

Even happy relationships don't always get everything right. Most of the couples we encountered had opposing attitudes, convictions, and occasionally clashing points of view regarding crucial issues.

Every marriage should have some strife. Successful, committed couples often made jokes about their differences and appreciated each other's opinions.

Keep in mind that one of the key components to keeping your marriage working is respect. Recognize that only one of two opposing viewpoints needs to be accurate.

8. Communicate

The Languages of Love is a topic that many books cover. This was born out of the psychological idea that every person shows love differently. You can use metaphors to express your opinions if you are aware of your spouse's interests and preferences.

How your spouse physically displays their devotion might help you determine whether or not your marriage is happy and healthy.

This may mean picking up the kids or washing your car. Two instances include ironing his clothes and replenishing the restroom with supplies. Others delight in words, literature, and romance. A good and healthy marriage requires that you are aware of your partner's love language.

9. Pardon one another

One of the most difficult lessons to learn might be this one, especially if you have a propensity for holding grudges. This key, along with praying and extending grace, is essential.

It takes time and patience with both yourself and your spouse to look at your spouse and tell them that you forgive them for hurting you in the past, but forgiveness could make your marriage keep working and growing stronger.

10. Acceptance

Lack of acceptance is a trait that is commonly associated with nagging women and is a major relationship killer. Keep in mind that you married your mate for who he was and is today. We can't change him right now, even if we wanted to.

This needs to be understood as soon as is practical to keep your marriage working on

You don't mention his flaws or issues when you press him or try to persuade him. As soon as you can, shift your attention to virtues.

11. Accept accountability

It is that simple, and it's one of the secrets to a happy and successful marriage. As you work on a project, take responsibility for your accomplishments and shortcomings.

When you and your partner disagree or argue, always keep in mind that you are responsible for everything you did and said, especially if it was unkind, negligent, or created problems.

12. Never assume anything about another person.
When individuals presume the best of one another, this is maybe the most hazardous pathogen of all. It is simple for a couple to become complacent and their expectations to raise once they feel at ease with one another.

It is inevitable for us to do so due to our intrinsic desire to get acclimated to the familiar. But you must never allow yourself to reach the point in a marriage where you start to take your spouse for granted.

13. Date night

Dating is the one aspect of enjoying a good and healthy marriage of which most couples either overlook or undervalue. Over time, spending time together even just one night a week deepens and sustains the relationship. Put your phones away and switch them off before going on a date to prevent being distracted.

Visit a hiking trail, try rollerblading, or watch a movie and have some popcorn at home. Be kind and supportive to one another, and switch things up often. There are many stages to a happy marriage, not simply a sweet and thoughtful date night.

To ensure responsibility and create a habit of prioritizing, it is essential to schedule date nights at least once every month.

14. Step up the chemistry

Do you want to find out how to keep your marriage working? Keep things simple and fundamental in your connection. One day, as simply two romantic gestures, consider bringing her flowers or concealing a love note in his luggage or briefcase. Send him a surprise dinner, or accompany him to watch the sunset.

There is no shortage of marriage advice, and you'd be surprised at how much romance can bolster a union.

15. Maintain privacy

A good and healthy marriage requires sexual intimacy. Therapists advise frequently having sex, even when you don't feel like it.

16. Accolades laud your partner.

Daily compliments and confirmations of your partner's good qualities can go a long way in your relationship. Keep a cheerful attitude and be aware of your partner's possessions.

Try shifting gears and highlighting his great qualities rather than focusing on his flaws when things become tough and his less than desirable attributes start to surface.

17. Search for a relaxing feeling
Compliment-your-spouse

Psychologists support the idea that every "hard" emotion is accompanied by a softer one. Typically, anger is merely the surface of another emotion, such as grief, disappointment, or envy. We typically cover up our inadequacies with our fury.

You will be able to relate to someone's true mood more if you search for the "soft" or sensitive feelings that are concealed behind their skilled outward display of rage.

We frequently look for advice on getting married and having a relationship. We keep missing the truth that knowing that emotions aren't always what they seem to be could point us on the proper route.

18. Let your desire of praising your man in every way come true.

Unfortunately, some of these misconceptions about reality may follow us into adulthood because we are taught that all stories have happy ends. While marriage might be lovely, it's important to understand that neither it nor it will ever be easy.

Keep your expectations in control and avoid believing in fairy tales since you can end up being disappointed. This is not just one of the most crucial components of a happy marriage, but it also has a significant impact on your contentment.

19. Don't try to be in charge.
Married people frequently go through a phase where they lose themselves, give in to inferiority or jealousy, forget that they are separate people from their spouses, and even feel the need to dominate them.

The majority of the time, this happens unintentionally because expectations might change over time.

The keys to keeping your marriage working include open communication, respect for each other's privacy, and occasional, healthy indulgences. Get a handle on it or schedule a meeting with a family counselor if you feel oppressed or in charge.

20. Do not use the D-word.

Do not threaten to divorce if you do not mean to. This can be used as a coping method by couples who mention the prospect of separation or use the D-word during arguments. It is more likely to occur when one partner threatens the other with divorce.

Avoid using threats as a means of conflict resolution because they are not a responsible strategy.

21. Lead everyone in prayer

Even amid your hectic days, one of those keys takes up so little time that you and your partner can still breathe together. Pray with your husband every night, either just before bed or shortly after you put the kids to sleep.

Give God thanks and spend some time being gracious to one another. Your emotional ties to both your spouse and God are strengthened when you include God in your marriage during these intimate moments.

22. Be patient with one another.

Making up with your spouse after a fight often requires making a deliberate choice.

Parenting books claim that kids commonly act out in front of their parents since that's where they feel safest and most at ease. This also holds for good and healthy marriages.

Because we feel safe and at ease with our spouses, we regularly display our most ugly sides to them. Typically, that conveys a significant deal of frustration and impatience. When they take an eternity to get ready or take longer than expected to get home, we become frustrated.

Keep in mind that this is the person you adore most of all. Treat them with the same patience you would your small child, at the very least.

23. Encourage one another.
It's critical to understand your partner's objectives. A wonderful opportunity to discuss your goals is at the start of the year. Encourage your partner to follow through on their goals and resolutions when they discuss them with you. Give both of your goals and theirs equal weight.

Be their utmost supporter, do everything in your power to assist them, and give them the room they require to achieve their yearly objectives. This also applies to the objectives you set together.

What you can do to help each other become your best selves is by motivating and inspiring one another, setting your goals and your spouse's goals in order, while also acknowledging your development.

www.ingramcontent.com/pod-product-compliance
Lightning Source LLC
LaVergne TN
LVHW020530160826
845677LV00015B/3991
* 9 7 9 8 8 4 4 0 1 0 8 1 1 *